CODING FOR KIDS
SCRATCH

A Step-by-Step Guide to Building Your First 10 Projects

by Nathan Jobs

© Copyright 2020 - All rights reserved.

The content contained within this book may not be reproduced, duplicated or transmitted without direct written permission from the author or the publisher.

Under no circumstances will any blame or legal responsibility be held against the publisher, or author, for any damages, reparation, or monetary loss due to the information contained within this book, either directly or indirectly.

Legal Notice:

This book is copyright protected. It is only for personal use. You cannot amend, distribute, sell, use, quote or paraphrase any part, or the content within this book, without the consent of the author or publisher.

Disclaimer Notice:

Please note the information contained within this document is for educational and entertainment purposes only. All effort has been executed to present accurate, up to date, reliable, complete information. No warranties of any kind are declared or implied. Readers acknowledge that the author is not engaged in the rendering of legal, financial, medical or professional advice. The content within this book has been derived from various sources. Please consult a licensed professional before attempting any techniques outlined in this book.

By reading this document, the reader agrees that under no circumstances is the author responsible for any losses, direct or indirect, that are incurred as a result of the use of the information contained within this document, including, but not limited to, errors, omissions, or inaccuracies.

Scratch is a project of the Scratch Foundation, in collaboration with the Lifelong Kindergarten Group at the MIT Media Lab. It is available for free at https://scratch.mit.edu

Table of Contents

Introduction 5
Chapter 1: Introduction to Programming 7
    What is Programming? 7
    Why Kids Should Learn Programming? 8
    Why Scratch? 9
    Answers To Important Questions 9
Chapter 2: Digital Legos 11
    What Are Blocks? 12
    Building Lego 13
Chapter 3: Start Scratching! 15
    Install and Setup 15
    Take Command, Peter Pan! 22
Chapter 4: Toolbox 39
    Events 39
    Control 42
    Sensors 43
Chapter 5: Merry Go Round 46
    Loop #1 47
    Loop #2 50
    Loop within a Loop 52
Chapter 6: Toy Box 54
Chapter 7: Breaking Stuff Is Good 59
    Data Race 59
    Variable Attribution 61
    Confusing Similar Blocks 61
    Wrong Placement 64
Chapter 8: Cartoons Are Cool 67
Chapter 9: Let's Dance 75

- Chapter 10: Become A Scientist 77
  - The Calculator 77
  - The Magician 79
  - Advanced Concepts 81
  - Health is Happiness 84
  - Project Ideas 87
- Conclusion 90

Introduction

Hey kiddo, this is your friendly neighborhood Spiderman! No? Yeah, you got me, I'm actually Nathan. You can call me Nat because I am also friendly (and a teensy-weensy bit funny). I am going to take you on an exciting adventure where you'll have fun and learn new things at the same time. Everyone thinks Harry Potter is so cool because he can do magic, but let me tell you a secret. You can do magic too, you just need to learn how to do it. There's more good news! You can do it without going to Hogwarts and leaving your friends and family!

I am going to teach you Scratch. You'll learn more about what it is later in this book, but here's a little secret: I have written this book so, except for a few parts where you'll need guidance or assistance from an adult, you can learn and do cool stuff without anyone's help! You can even team up with your friends or challenge them to complete projects in this book. How cool is that? Cooler than slurpees, in my opinion!

Hey kid, right now, if you are reading this book all by yourself, you might want to ask an adult to stick around to answer any questions from here on until we reach Chapter 2. I know it's not very cool, but we might need their help installing something on the computer so you can start doing magic! I promise, they won't be needed for the whole book and you can hush them away when we move on to the fun part.

Hey adult, the kid might need your help until he or she reaches chapter 2. So, hang around and help them learn some amazing stuff! By the way, thanks for letting your child read this book. If you are still not sure why every kid should read it and learn coding, let me explain the dilemma.

In today's world it is really important for kids to identify and hone their creative side. It will immensely help them when they grow up and look to do adult things such as finding a job. Our world is changing fast and professional skills of the past are becoming obsolete every day. Everything is being automated, everyday management and operational jobs are getting scarce, and it will be worse when the kids grow up. But, do you know what machines won't be able to ever replace? Human creativity. That mind, the feelings, that heart, and the things that make us human! You might see burger flipping machines at McDonalds in the coming years, but you won't be seeing a machine making the perfect home-cooked meal a mother can cook up in the kitchen. You know what makes it taste so much better? It's the *"being human and loved"* feeling that meal gives you that makes all the difference. That's what will matter in the future, in the era of machines.

You might be wondering why your child has to use a computer to not be like a computer? I always encourage kids to be surrounded by parents, family and friends because kids learn the fastest by observation. What they see adults doing when they are young will shape how they behave when they grow up. But, unfortunately, our society and lifestyles aren't affording us all these things. Kids these days are also spending a lot of time with smart devices, so why not use that opportunity to have them learn something useful and still have fun? So yes, it is not the ideal solution, but this is you making the best of the circumstances. I have written this book so it's much more enjoyable with friends, so please do encourage your kid to read this book and do the projects with their friends. If they ask you if they can do that, even better.

This book is divided into several chapters, each focusing on only one topic. You should supervise your child through chapter one because they might need your help in installing the correct software and in rare circumstances, also need help in getting used to the computer and software. Kids are quick learners, so I am confident they won't need you all the time. Chapter two is all theory and explains one base concept. If you have already supervised through chapter one, chapter three wouldn't require your attention as they should be able to find and install the software themselves. If they still need help, please make sure they are not left unattended for a long time as that might make them frustrated and lose interest. Remember, kids have very small attention spans. Chapter three also has the first project. All subsequent chapters will have one or more projects that they can do all by themselves or with friends to make it more fun. The projects cover various fields and you should keep an eye out for how they reacted to different projects. It might help you recognize interests, strengths, and weaknesses.

Make sure to read the conclusion together as well. It has pointers for you to see what your child thought about the book and what to do next. Every kid is different. Some might find this book amazing, while some might hate it. It is completely understandable, and the idea of this book is not to be liked necessarily, but to fuel the creative mind and spark a response.

One last thing I would advise is to have an open mind when interpreting a child's response to this book or to anything else. Creativity at such a tender age can translate into many different yet amazing things in later years. I still remember when I was so good with paintings, I was really creative, temperamental and expressive in my early ages. Today, I am a full-time programmer who loves solving complex problems with fresh creativity. My oldest son, Kyle, loves to make sand castles. I get excited and nervous about what that might translate to in the future. It's fun in its own way, isn't it? Let's teach every kid something that will help them for the rest of their lives.

Chapter 1: Introduction to Programming

Hey kid. Hello, yes, you there. It's me, Nat again! Let me ask you something.

What's the best thing that ever happened to you? Think hard, because it is important.

Was it the first birthday party you remember? Was it when you made your first friend? Was it when mommy hugged you and said she loves you more than anything? Was it your dad telling you the best bed-time story ever?

It was definitely not your first day at school (if it is, you are very lucky, believe me). I am sure that you love that moment because it makes you happy. I can tell you what is the best thing that ever happened to computers. It was programming. Well, it doesn't make computers happy (because they can't feel anything!), but they made people who work with computers very happy. So, what is programming?

What is Programming?

Programming is the way humans tell machines what to do (much like how your mom tells your dad what needs to be done!). They are a group of instructions that people write and feed into machines, then the machines read them, understand what needs to be done, perform the required actions, and output the desired results. A simplified definition is: "giving instructions to a computer to perform some task."

We also use the word "coding" instead of programming, for the simple reason that programs are also called codes. It is very common in real-life to have two, three or more words that mean the same. Many people have nicknames or alternate names. Do you know if you have one? Time to ask around!

If you think about it, everyone does some kind of *programming* in real life, either when they are interacting with machines or other people. The purpose of programming might differ, but they do it even without knowing about it. Next time you see someone telling another person or machine what to do, you would know they are a programmer!

But, if everyone does programming in real-life, why are they not able to program computers? There is a very simple reason. You need to know the language of computers. Yes, it's just like English, which helps you communicate with everyone else. Computers have their own language and programmers have to learn it before they can start programming. By the way, did you know English is the most spoken language by humans in the world? Do you know which is the second most important language in the world? Go find out!

But, there's a problem. Computers communicate through numbers. It's what makes them so much faster than humans. A lot of humans are very bad with numbers. Have you ever memorized number tables? You must know how difficult it is to remember them. Decades ago, programmers used to code in numbers so computers could understand the instructions. But, some smart people invented programming languages that enabled people to use words and phrases from human languages to write a program. With time, improvements were made and programming languages became easier. Today, we have stuff like Scratch that enables kids like you to program fun things without much of a problem.

Why Kids Should Learn Programming?

I know you must be wondering why you should read this book and not go watch a cartoon like Spongebob or Spiderman. Or maybe play a game? Well, here's a question for you: is it better to watch a cartoon or build one of your own? How about creating a game of your own that you can play by your own rules? Sounds fantastic, doesn't it? Perhaps you challenge your friends to try and beat you...how much fun that would be! If you stick with this book, you will be able to do all of these things and more.

In the introduction to this book, I have already talked about the topic of why kids should learn programming. Here's another serious reason: kids can explore their creative side without the need for big financial investment or the need to go somewhere else. Truth be told, kids these days also have a busy schedule. Taking kids out on school days to somewhere that they can focus on a new thing isn't feasible for most kids or their parents.

Most homes have access to computers and the Internet, so they can be utilized for kids without any new investment. The software is completely free, so there's no need to allocate gas money or take time out of your schedule for pick up and drop off. You could be cooking a meal or catching up on pending tasks while your kid is learning new things and remaining within your reach.

Why Scratch?

With this book, kids will learn to use Scratch, a free programming software used to complete fun projects. Scratch is designed for kids and offers an engaging, interactive, visual interface to achieve desired results. Kids do not write program instructions, they manipulate visual objects so there's no need to learn any dedicated programming language. Learning how to use Scratch in itself is quite a fun and engaging experience.

It is important to note that Scratch is not the only visual programming software available. There are advanced options like Tynker that kids can use to create awesome games. But, it is not free and is better for kids who already have some basic programming knowledge. Scratch is free and relatively basic so kids do not have a steep learning curve.

Answers To Important Questions

I understand that as an adult responsible for a kid, you must have many questions about the Scratch software. Where do I access the software? Is it safe for my kid? Can I install it on my cell phone and can I choose when my kid uses the software? Can a stranger interact with them through the software? In this section, I will try to give as much information as possible to answer all such questions.

Requirements

The following things are needed to learn Scratch and start programming with this book.
- This book (very funny, I know!)
- Access to a working computer or a mobile device such as smartphone or a tablet
- Uninterrupted Internet service (if using the online version of Scratch) with correct parental controls
- Stationery like a notebook, along with a pencil, eraser, etc.
- Adult supervision during installation (and uninstallation)

This book is written with the assumption that we are working on a desktop computer using a Windows operating system. But, as listed above, you can use any other computer system or device.

Safety and Security

It is your responsibility to implement proper parental controls on the computer and Internet service so the online experience is safe for your kid. If you are unfamiliar with parental controls, I advise you to learn about them at the first chance you get and implement them on all devices that are accessible to kids. In this book, I have assumed that's already taken care of before giving kids access to the computer and Internet.

Scratch software is designed for kids and utmost care has been given by developers and moderators to keep the software and the related online community safe and secure for kids. Scratch was developed as a free project by a team of developers at MIT through collaboration with a Canadian firm. Over the years, the number of users has grown from a few dozens to hundreds of thousands worldwide and is still growing every day.

Exposure

Scratch is available as an online tool as well as an offline downloadable software. I would suggest downloading and installing the software on your computer. It gives you two important advantages:

1. Kids can use the software even when the Internet is out

2. You can deliberately turn off the Internet in the device the kid is using for Scratch so you have the surety they won't be exposed to questionable material over the Internet even by accident

If you have more questions, you can always visit the online community of Scratch and find answers. I am sure you will find answers to every possible concern you might have. When ready, give your kid the thumbs up to continue with this book! It's time for magic!

Chapter 2: Digital Legos

Do you like Legos? I loved Legos when I was a kid, and I still love them. I think everyone loves Legos. They are so much fun (though not so much fun for moms who have to clean up after kids are done with them). You can build really cool things by putting Lego pieces together, just like the kid who is trying to build something in the picture below.

Kid playing with lego

Do you have a Lego set? Recall what you can build with the set. I used to own a very small police Lego set. Even though it was small, it was a complex set because I had to construct a watch tower using Lego pieces. I had to understand various shapes and how they can fit together because many pieces looked almost the same. Have you ever seen twin kids that look almost the same but are two different people? It is so hard to know which one is which. It took me weeks to figure out the Lego set. I still have the Lego set in my basement after all these years.

Scratch is just like playing with Lego pieces, it's just on a computer. You build something by putting pieces together, making sure you are connecting the right ones.

What Are Blocks?

Blocks are a real-life concept. You might have seen white walls made of concrete blocks just like in the picture below. They are usually used in high-rise buildings. Have you visited any high-rise building? In most countries, a high-rise building is a very tall building with more than 7 floors!

Concrete blocks are similar in concept to red bricks but have different characteristics. Red bricks are more common in Western countries because they are great at keeping a house warm. Concrete blocks are bulkier and much stronger so they are ideal for tall buildings.

A wall made of concrete blocks

Blocks In Programming

In Scratch programming, each piece you put together to create stuff is called a block. This approach to programming is therefore called block-oriented programming. You must put the right blocks together to create something meaningful. Depending on the situation, you must also change the setting of some or all of the blocks to get the desired results. This book will teach you the entire process. In short, you will become Bob the Builder who scratches!

Building Lego

Let us see how we build something using a Lego set.

Things we need

Let's create a list of everything we need.

1. A complete Lego set. We won't be able to fully build the desired construction if parts are missing.
2. A picture of the completed construction. This helps us to know if we have put everything together the right way.
3. The Lego set also comes with instructions and the sequence on how to build using that set. You must follow the instructions in the correct sequence to complete the build.

Build

Here is a step-by-step guide on how to build using a Lego set.

1. Identify all the different pieces (we also call them bricks) in the Lego set.

2. If there are too many bricks, divide them into several heaps by grouping similar bricks together.

3. Using the instructions, start building in the given sequence. I know skipping a few steps sounds tempting, but do not skip a step. It will make things difficult down the line.

4. Once the construction is built, pose like a king because you truly deserve it, and maybe some pizza!

Using Scratch to build stuff is very similar to building things with Lego sets. In both situations, it is very important to follow the sequence. Here's some Gandalf wisdom for you: shortcuts are never good, not in real-life and not while programming. If you do not know who Gandalf is, well, that needs to be corrected right away!

Chapter 3: Start Scratching!

Kid, it is time we have some adventure, action and fun. Do you have permission to install something on the home computer or the smart device you usually use? If yes, you should follow the next sections to install and setup Scratch. If not, you need help from an adult again. Sorry, I know, I promise this is the last time!

Install and Setup

There are two ways we can use Scratch

- Online platform
- Offline software (preferred)

Online Platform

The official link to the Scratch website is https://scratch.mit.edu/. Open up a web browser on your device. In this book we have used Google Chrome. The website will look like the picture below.

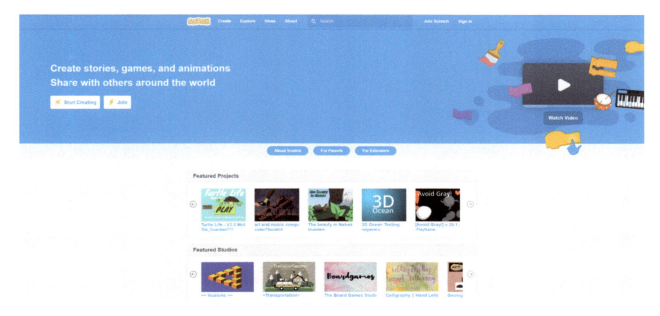

If you want to start building projects right away, click on "Create" at the top menu.

Creating an account will allow you to share projects with others and make friends online in a safe, regulated online community! Click on "Join Scratch" to create a Scratch account. It is absolutely free.

The sign-up form gives helpful prompts to explain the sign-up process. Please make sure to write down the password and place it somewhere safe. Remember that online account passwords must never be shared with anyone under any circumstances. Modern browsers have the option to save the login details, which makes subsequent logins convenient and faster. You can also benefit from that feature.

The sign up form will initially look like the screenshot below.

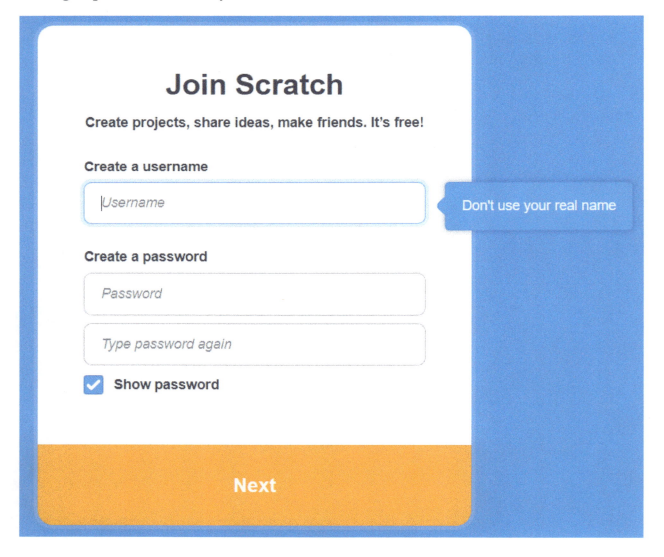

Click on "Next" after filling in username and password. The username cannot be changed later and is used to identify users on Scratch platform, so make sure it is something you will love.

Next, you will be asked about the country you are located in. I live in the United States, so I chose that.

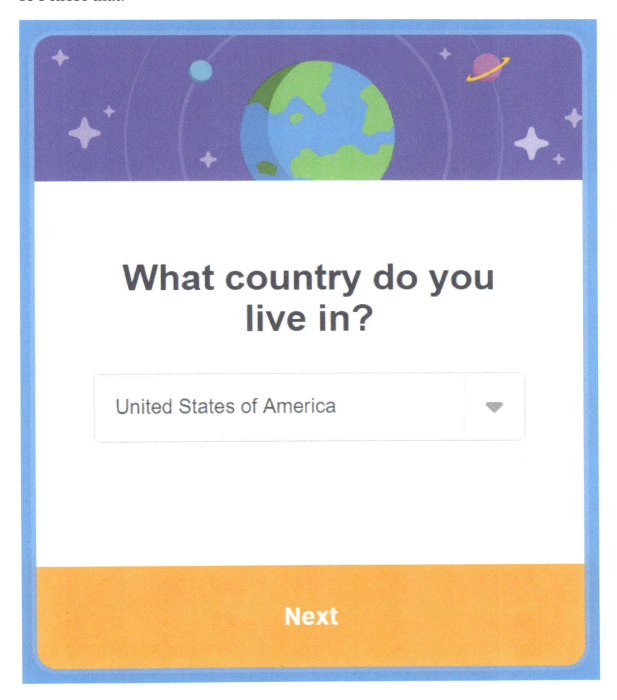

Then it's your birthday. Make sure you use the correct date for the birthday. In case you forget the password, usually this piece of information is requested to verify if it is really you.

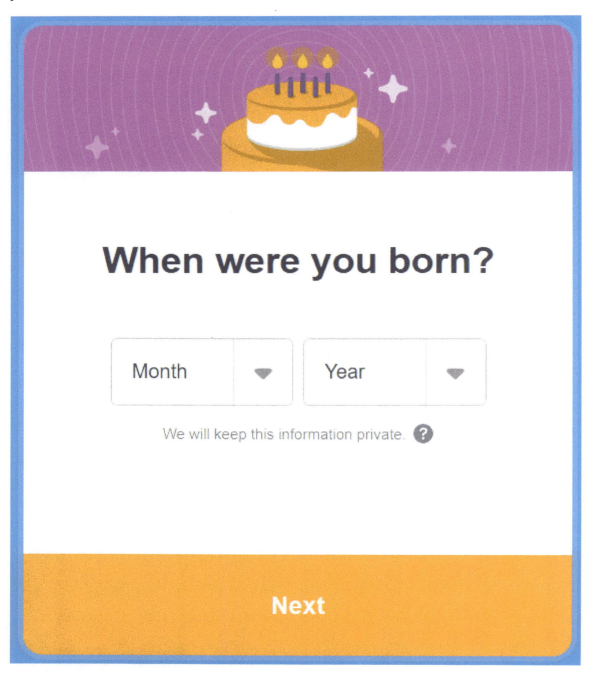

The next screen will ask about gender. Select the appropriate option.

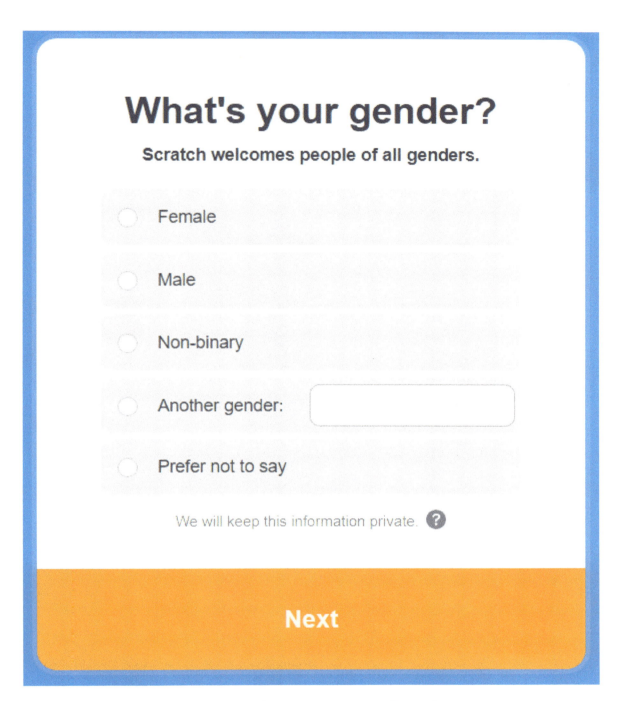

An email ID is required in the last step to complete sign up. Most common email services like Gmail do not allow accounts for anyone younger than 13 years old. However, there are many kids-friendly email services such as Zillamail that have built-in profanity filters offering a safe email service to kids. On the flipside, most such services are paid. Alternatively, you can use your parent's email ID to complete the sign up.

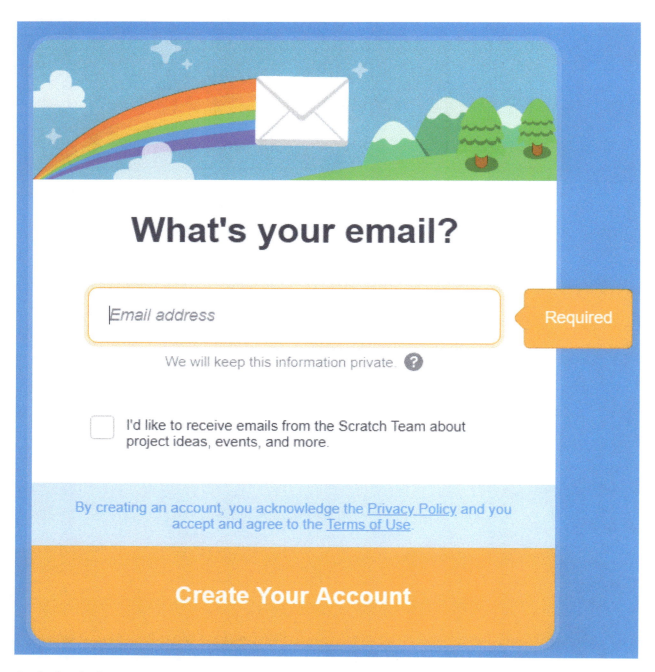

And that's it! You can start using the online version of Scratch to create and share Scratch projects. Scratch will send a confirmation link to the email address provided during sign up. Don't forget to click on the link in the email to confirm your account.

Offline Application (Preferred)

You do not need to sign up for an account to use the Scratch application on your own computer. The downside is, you will not be able to share your projects with others on the Internet. But, this option is better for kids like you who want to become a master.

On a Windows operating system, there are two ways to install the offline version of Scratch.

Download Installer from Scratch Website

To download and install the Scratch application on your computer, use the download link: https://scratch.mit.edu/download. Choose the Operating System (OS) that your computer uses. Windows is selected by default. Note that at least Windows 10 is required for Scratch to work.

Install from Windows Store

If you have a Windows 10 based computer, you can also install the Scratch application through the Microsoft store. Click on the "Windows" logo in the bottom left corner of your screen. In the search bar type "Microsoft Store" and select the first option. In the new application window, you will see the "Search" option towards the top right-hand corner. Search for "Scratch" and you will see "Scratch Desktop" as the very first option.

Select the option and then you can install the application.

No matter how you installed the application, the Scratch application can be accessed from the start menu. Please note that sometimes applications on Windows Store are not readily updated. If you installed Scratch from Windows Store and it gives a fatal error when you run the application, uninstall it and download the installer from Scratch website. For easier access for kids, create a desktop shortcut for the application.

Take Command, Peter Pan!

Hey kid, Nat's back with you and good news, no more adults and we are all set up to have fun! I have to ask you a question. Do you know who Peter Pan is? Yes? Good job smarty-pants. Well, let me tell you anyways, because I also have a secret to share.

Peter Pan is an independent, confident, free-spirited kid who can fly, do magic stuff, goes on adventures, helps other kids, and stands against evil. He's also a bit naughty, which is good, right? He also leads other kids so they can also be good and have fun. You know what's the sad part? Everyone thinks Peter Pan is not real.

But, I know a secret no one else knows and I can't hold onto it any longer. Let me spill it out. You, Mr. Smarty-pants, are Peter Pan! Well, I know you can't fly, but you can do everything else that Peter Pan could, and some more! You can use Scratch to make amazing things. Let's dive in!

Things-That-Must-Not-Be-Done!

Peter Pan is nearly invincible, but even he must be wary of a few things that can hurt really bad. I am giving you a list of things you must never do when using Scratch or anything on the Internet.

1. Never share the account password with anyone. This is a golden rule for every account made on the Internet.

2. Never interact with strangers.

3. Never share personal details with anyone on the Internet. Personal details include your name, contact information such as phone number and where you live. If you think it is important to share, discuss with an adult in your house so they can decide if it's really necessary.

4. Never close Scratch application without saving the project (later I will tell you how to save your progress on Scratch).

5. Never hide if you experienced something on the Internet that made you uncomfortable. Share with your parents so they can protect you.

6. We, humans, have our limitations. For example, we can't fly on our own (because humans do not possess the physical requirements needed to fly). So, what would happen if someone tried to fly without using an airplane? They would fall (yikes) and it would be a very unpleasant sight. Just like humans, every machine and every application has some limits. Scratch is no exception, so, we must be aware of them and not exceed the limitations or things can become wonky.

7. Never leave the computer unattended and unlocked. Pee breaks are important, but before you leave, save your Scratch project and lock the computer. The last thing you want is your younger siblings making a mess or someone shutting down the computer!

8. Scratch does not have an UNDO feature, so a good idea is to plan ahead. Never start a project without thinking it through. With practice, you won't be needing to make a lot of changes.

9. Never be shy of making mistakes. Mistakes are fun because they are easy to remember and help you learn new things.

10. And the most important thing, because it is the hardest of all: Never give up! Things (like life in general) can be hard sometimes. You will be stuck, but never accept loss. If at first you don't succeed, try, try, try again!

The Concept of Give and Take

Have you ever gone to the mall with your parents or to the grocery store? You must have noticed how your parents hand out money or swipe their cards and, in exchange, the shopkeeper lets them keep whatever they gathered. Everything in the world works like this. You have to *give* something to *get* something.

Programming works on the same principles. You write a code/program that gives instructions to the computer. The computer processes and you get a response. In the computer world, what you give to the computer we call "input" and the response we get is called "output".

Now, here's when things can get confusing, so pay attention kiddo: programs are written for someone else to use them (we call them "users"). The user will use the program to do some work, in short giving input and getting output. This is how the entire world of the Internet works. Actually, this is also how the real world works. For example, talking about cars, they are made by people working in factories. People buy them and use them to go to work, to shop, and to have fun, like going to picnics.

You are going to be the Peter Pan of programmers. You are going to create stuff that others can use and have fun and learn new things at the same time.

Scratch Basics

Start Scratch

Let's start Scratch. Below are instructions for you on how to start Scratch.

- Click on the Scratch application icon on the desktop. The icon looks like this:

- Scratch will open up. It will look like this. What an amazing colorful screen! Do not worry if things on this new screen do not make sense to you right now. We are going to explain each section very soon.

Understanding different sections of Scratch screen

Menu Bar

The first thing you will notice is the blue line at the top with a bunch of options (the bunch of options is called a menu). The blue area is a long and stretched rectangle (like a bar), hence we call this whole area the menu bar.

- The first option in the blue menu bar is the logo of Scratch. Click on it with your mouse and you will see information about the Scratch application. I see this:

- The second option on the menu, represented by the icon of the world, is the "language" used in the Scratch application. You can change the language anytime you want. At the start, it is set to English.
- The third option is named "File", to be honest due to a lack of a better name! This is an option you will find in the menus of almost every application and it contains general but important actions. In Scratch, the "File" contains the following options (I will explain these options in a bit).

- The fourth option is "Edit". It has only two options and we will not be using any of them in this book. However, I will explain them, just for your curiosity!

- The fifth option is the "Tutorials" where you will find projects that you can run to understand different things about Scratch. No need to worry about them, as you have me and this book!
- The last option is a field where you can give a name to your current project. It might already be filled with "Scratch Project", but you can change it to whatever you like.

As promised, I am going to briefly explain the options you see after clicking on "File" or "Edit".

"File" Options

New: Use this option to create a new project. If you have already worked on a current project and haven't saved the changes, you will be reminded with a prompt. See, even Scratch knows how forgetful we are!

Load from your computer: You can load an already saved project using this option. You will need to remember where you saved your project and what the project name was.

Save to your computer: I know how important it is to take a bathroom break, or go eat cookies. You can do both without any worries because you can save your project using this option. Scratch will ask where to save the project and what to name it. Try to save it somewhere you will remember. I usually just select "Desktop". The name you gave to your project is automatically given to the filename.

"Edit" Options

Restore: If you deleted something by accident and want it back, you can use this option. Beware that this is **not** an UNDO button, so it will not revert everything you do in Scratch.

Turn on Turbo Mode: If your project has a lot of complex calculations, activate this mode and the projects may run faster.

Tabs

You will see three tabs on the Scratch screen like this:

We will learn about the three tabs in greater detail in the next chapters. For now, you should know their purpose.

"Code" Tab

This is where you will find all the blocks you can use to create projects. The blocks are grouped together by their type such as "motion", "looks" and "sound".

"Costumes" Tab

This tab gives you options to customize the look and behavior of characters in your project.

"Sounds" Tab

If you have used a sound block in your project, here you will be able to customize each sound component.

Controls

In the same line as the tabs, but towards the right side of your screen, you will see the following buttons.

Green flag

This runs your project

Red sign

This stops your project from running.

Turbo Mode

You see this if you have enabled the Turbo Mode from the Edit option in the menu bar.

View Options

The next three options change the look of the entire Scratch screen.

Stage

This is where you will see how your project runs. Every project starts with the cat character, so that's what we see on the stage.

Sprites and backdrops

We are going to learn two new words - sprites and backdrops.

Sprites

Sprites are objects that you can add to your object. The blocks we choose from the code tab are applied to these sprites.

Backdrop

These are the backgrounds we can choose for our projects.

First Project

Our cat, Mona, is hungry. In our first project, we will enable Mona to go near Abby, and demand some food! Well, Mona would just say "meow" but Abby will know what Mona wants. We all know what cats want - food!

Let's add Mona and Abby to our project "First Project". Here is how to do that.

1. To rename this project, click on the field beside Tutorials in the menu bar and type in "First Project".

2. Our cat will already be added to the project. We have to move the cat towards the bottom left side of the stage. On the stage, click and drag on the cat to move it.
3. Towards the bottom right hand corner of your screen, in the "sprites and backdrops" section, hover your mouse on the icon that looks like a cat icon (it will say "Choose a Sprite") and a blue strip will slide up. Select the first icon from the bottom that looks like a magnifying glass (that's the icon usually used to say "search").

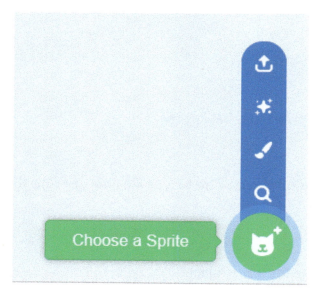

4. You will see a new window with a lot of characters. Select the one that says "Abby".

Now, in the "sprites and backdrops" section, you will see two sprites.

You will notice that Abby is selected because her icon has a thick blue border. We have to flip her so she faces toward the west. Click on the "Direction" and change the direction of the arrow so it points toward the west. Also, click on the *"arrow heads"* icon in the middle. On the next page, I have given before and after images to avoid any confusion.

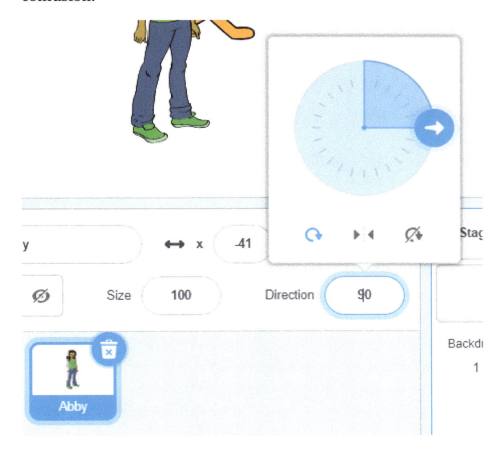

Before

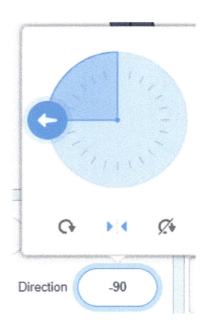

After

We also have to rename our cat.

In the "sprites and backdrops" section, click on the cat icon so it becomes highlighted. In the field that says "Sprite", change '*Sprite1*' to *Mona* (Press the ENTER key on your keyboard after you type Mona for the change to take effect). After the edit, the two sprites should look like this.

We also need to change the backdrop. Towards the bottom right hand corner of your screen, in the "sprites and backdrops" section, hover your mouse on the icon that looks like an image icon (it will say "Choose a Backdrop") and a blue strip will slide up. Select the first icon from the bottom that looks like a magnifying glass.

You will see a new window with a lot of backdrops. Select the one that says "Bedroom 1".

One last thing we need to do is move the sprites to correct locations.

Click on Mona, and in the box "x", enter -184. In the "y" box, enter -126.

x -184   y -126

Click on Abby, then enter 29 in the box "x", and enter -76 in the "y" box.

After all this work, the stage will look like this:

Now, it is time to give instructions to Mona using blocks so it can move towards Abby and demand some food.

In the "sprites and backdrops" section, make sure Mona is selected. From the code tab, select the "Events" option. You will see the block that says "when 🏁 clicked". Drag it to the workspace. In our book, almost every project will start with this block. It makes the project run when we click the green flag on the Scratch screen.

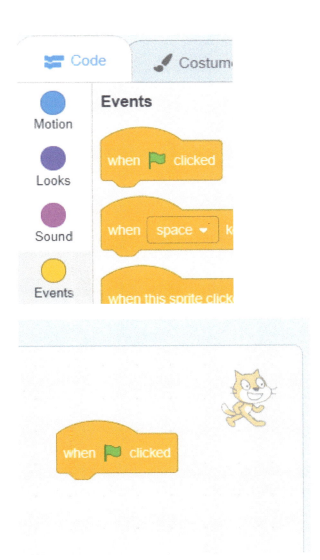

The block in the workspace, the washed-out cat icon, tells us that we are working with the cat Sprite

Now, select the "Motion" option in the code tab. You should be able to see the "move 10 steps" block.

Drag the block to the workspace so it stacks down with the previous block. Click on the blue block where it says "10" and change it to "150" steps. Your blocks should now look like this.

35

Linking blocks like this means they will be run one after the other.

Now, we need to give Mona a voice. Select the "Sound" option in the Code tab, then drag the "start sound Meow" block and stack it with the remaining blocks.

The blocks will look like this now.

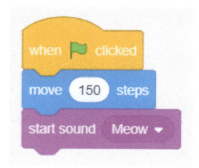

We need to add some text so everyone can know what *Meow* means. Let's go to the "Looks" option in the Code tab and drag the "say Hello! for 2 seconds" block to link with other blocks.

The blocks should look like this.

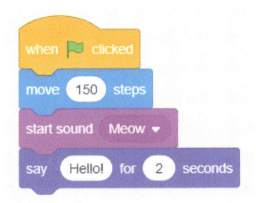

We also need to change the last block's settings (the purple block). Click where it says "Hello!" and change the text to "I need food!". Change the "2" seconds to "1". After you are done, the blocks should look like this.

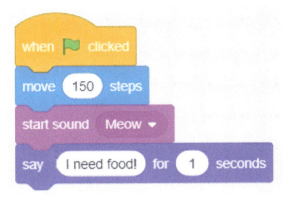

Our project is complete. We just need to save it and run it. Click on "File" in the menu bar and select the save option. Name the project file "First Project". If Scratch asks to replace another file with the same name, do it.

Ready to see something amazing? My heart is racing with excitement. Let's click on the green flag next to the red sign.

The cat will move closer to Abby, there will be a meow sound, and a popup will say, "I need food!"

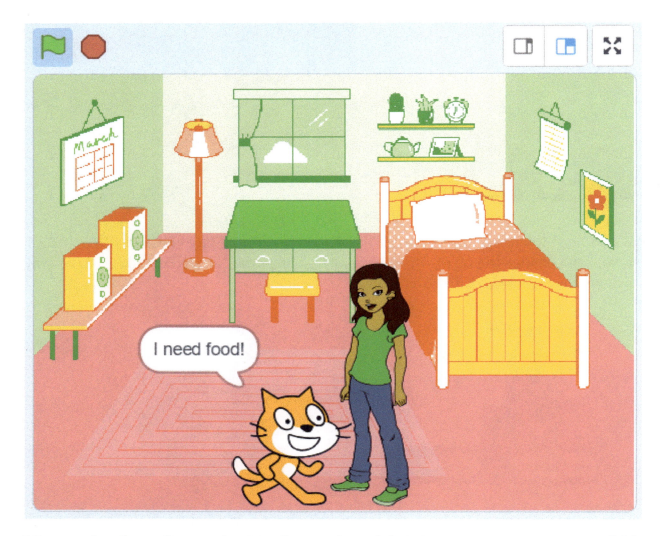

We completed our first project! Feels amazing, right? Our cat Mona was successful in telling Abby she's hungry and Abby is a good girl so she'll get Mona some food right away. Everybody wins!

In this chapter, we learned how to install and set up Scratch. We learned about the different parts of the Scratch screen and we also made our first cute project. Peter Pan, it's time for our next big thing: toy boxes.

Chapter 4: Toolbox

Every household has a toolbox. Let me rephrase: every dad has a toolbox even though mom says they can't fix anything! But, dads love toolboxes because according to them, they have important tools that can be used to fix or create.

We can say Scratch is a toolbox, too! It has a lot of tools (which we call blocks) that we can use to create amazing stuff. In this chapter, we are going to take a look at a couple of these amazing tools.

Events

We have already used one "events" option in our first project. Let's use another one in a project where the cat will meow and move 10 steps to the right whenever the RIGHT

ARROW key is pressed. Also, the cat should meow and move 10 steps to the left whenever the LEFT ARROW key is pressed.

We will start with dragging the "when SPACE is pressed" block from the "Events" option under Code tab to the workspace. Change the SPACE to RIGHT ARROW. Add the "move 10 steps" and "start sound MEOW" blocks so the stack looks like below.

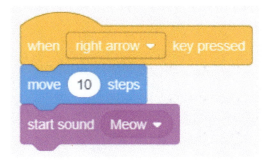

Now, we duplicate this block stack by right-clicking and selecting "Duplicate".

In the duplicated stack, change the RIGHT ARROW to LEFT ARROW and change the 10 steps to -10 steps. The entire workspace should look like this now.

As you can see, these are two separate, independent block stacks. Therefore, they run independently of each other. I added a wall backdrop to make it look better.

To run this project, we don't have to press the green flag. Press LEFT ARROW or RIGHT ARROW key and the sprite cat will respond accordingly. Here's the stage screenshot where I added a wall backdrop.

Want to know a secret? Spam the arrow keys and see how funny the cat looks and sounds!

Control

When we write programs, many times we have to enable our program to make decisions. We do it all the time in real life. Let me know how familiar this situation is: If mommy is happy, ask for cookies, else if mommy is angry, give her a hug. If mommy becomes happy, ask for cookies!

Every human is making decisions all the time. If this happens, do this, else do this. We can add this capability to our programs, too. In the "Code" tab, click on the orange "Control" option. You will see the following two blocks:

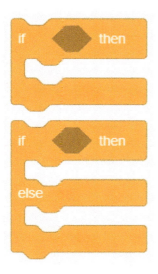

These two blocks represent what we call "conditionals". We can use any of them, the only difference is the second block has an ELSE branch as well. They check a condition, and if it's true, it executes the blocks inside IF branch. If the condition turns out to be false, the blocks inside the ELSE branch execute.

We are going to use the conditional blocks in the next section when we create our very own Hunger game, where our cat Mona is hungry again!

Sensors

In a visual programming platform like Scratch, it is very important to sense various events happening so we can use them as a trigger for something else. For example, we can sense when one sprite touches another sprite so we can start a sound. Let's create the Hunger Games for our cat Mona where you have to guide her to a milk carton using the ARROW keys on the keyboard. When Mona touches the milk she will say *Meow*.

Create a new project, name it "Second Project" and add a bedroom backdrop. I have used the "Bedroom 2" backdrop. Now, add two sprites:

1. Cat
2. Milk

Select the "Milk" sprite and change its size to 50 and change the x and y values to 199 and 60.

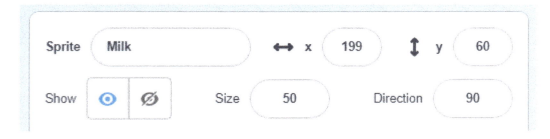

Now, select the "Cat" sprite, and add the blocks as given in the following order.

1. Add the "when SPACE is pressed" block in the "Events" in the Code tab. Change it so SPACE is replaced by RIGHT ARROW.

2. Now add the block "change x by 10"

3. Add the IF conditional block in the "Control" option of the Code tab.

4. In the empty box, place a "touching MOUSE-POINTER" block. Change MOUSE-POINTER to MILK

5. Inside the IF conditional block, place the "start sound MEOW" block from the "Sound" option from the Code tab.

After you are done, the whole block stack will look like this:

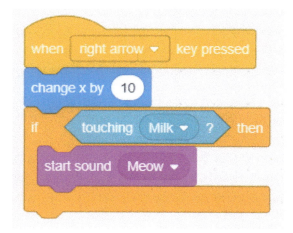

Let's duplicate this stack for all the ARROW keys. For the UP and DOWN arrows, use the "change y by 10" block. You will have four block stacks and your workspace should look like this.

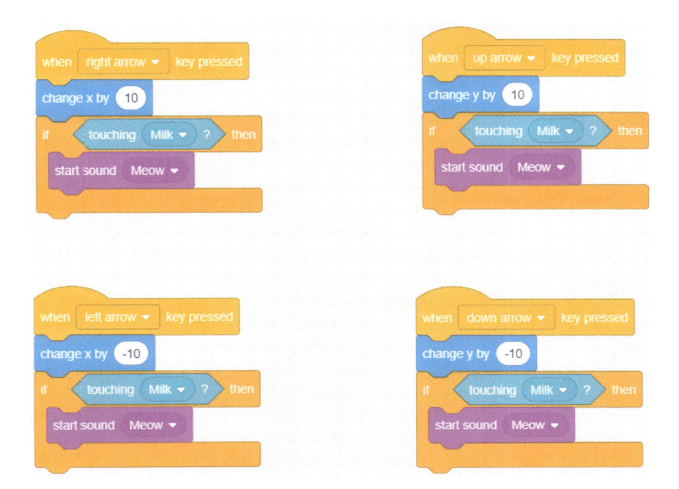

This is all we have to do. Our very own Hunger game is ready! Play around with the ARROW keys and guide our cat Mona to the milk carton. Each time she touches the milk carton, she'll *MEOW* with happiness. You'll love it!

Chapter 5: Merry Go Round

Have you been to a circus or a local festival where they have rides and things for everyone? Or you might have seen one on TV. The fancier merry-go-rounds have horse rides that also move up and down as you go around in circles. It was one of the things I loved the most when I was a kid. It was all fun and not scary at all! The ride goes round and round and round, endlessly and it has just the right speed.

In programming, we also have things that go round, round, and round! They are called loops. Yes, just loops, not the froot loops everyone loves! With loops we can do one or more tasks several times.

There are essentially two kinds of loops:

1. Loops that run for a specific number of times. We set the counter when creating the loop.

2. Loops that run until a specific condition is met. We define that condition when creating the loop.

We are going to work on two projects in this chapter. Each project will focus on one type of the loop.

Loop #1

Have you ever taken a ride in a helicopter? Helicopters are so cool and scary at the same time. I loved helicopters. I have never been on a helicopter but as a kid, I used to be a helicopter enthusiast. I collected helicopter models and read books about them. I think I was inspired by the 80s TV show *Airwolf*. Okay, let me be clear. I am not *that* old and there's nothing wrong with watching very old TV shows, especially when they are as unique as *Airwolf*.

You know what's even cooler than helicopters? Spaceships! The first time I saw a spaceship was in a movie. I don't remember what the name of the movie was but it made a lasting impression on me. Well, not everyone can go on spaceships. Technology is still not that advanced! But, that doesn't mean we can't imagine hopping onto a spaceship and cruising along an alien planet's surface. You know what, let's do that!

Create a new project, name it "Third Project" and add a backdrop named "Space". Add a "Rocketship" sprite. Make sure it is selected in the "sprite and backdrop" section and change the direction of the sprite to 139:

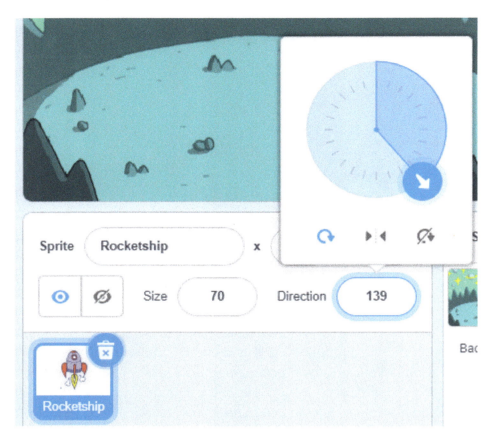

Now, making sure the "Rocketship" sprite is still selected, start adding the following blocks (in the exact same order):

1. Add "when 🏁 clicked" block from the "Events" options in the Code tab.
2. Add "go to x:124 y:107" block from the "Motion" options in the Code tab. Change the x value to -176 and y value to 107.
3. Now, from "Control" options in the same Code tab, add the block that looks like this (change the 10 to 70):

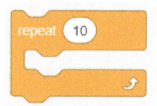

4. Inside the jaw of the above loop block, place a "change x by 10" block which is found in the "Motion" options in the Code tab. Change the 10 to 8.
5. From the "Sound" options in Code tab, drag the "start sound *space ripple*" and place it inside the loop block after the motion block.

The final stack will look like the image below.

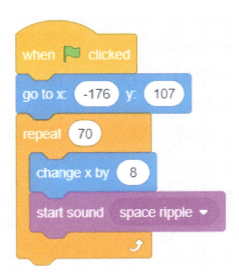

The stage may look like this before running the project:

Now, run your project by clicking on the green flag and see the spaceship speed through the night sky of this alien planet with very mysterious sci-fi sound effects!

Loop #2

The loop we used in the previous project will run 70 times because we set that value in the loop. What if we don't know the exact number when creating the loop? For example, if you run the above project, you will see that the spaceship actually flies off the screen. What if we want to run the loop until our sprite touches the edge of the stage?

Let's see how we can do that. Let me introduce my health-conscious friend, Avery, who needs our guidance while walking around the city streets. Let's create a fun little project to help Avery walk on city streets without wandering out too far.

Let's create a new project. If the previous project is still open, make sure to save it before creating a new project. Name the new project "Fourth Project" and start making the following changes.

1. Choose the "Colorful City" backdrop.
2. Select the "Avery Walking" sprite. Change the size to 40. Change the x and y values to x: -220 and y: -123. The sprite setting should look like this.

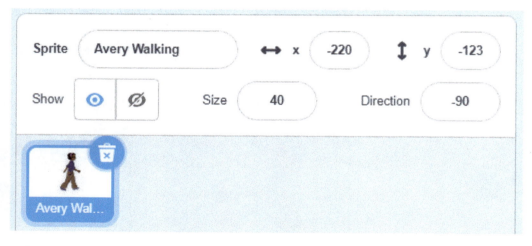

Now, we have to add some blocks to this Avery.

1. Add "point in direction 90" block from the "Motion" options in the Code tab.
2. Add "go to x:124 y:107" block from the "Motion" options in the Code tab. Change the x value to -213 and y value to -123.
3. Now, from "Control" options in the same Code tab, add the block that looks like this:

4. In the hollow box of this loop block, put the block "touching MOUSE-POINTER" block. Change MOUSE-POINTER to EDGE.
5. Inside the same loop block, add a "change x by 10" block from "Motion" options under the Code block. Change 10 to 2.

The block stack should look like this.

Now, we need to duplicate this whole block. Right click on this and select "Duplicate". It will create another block stack. Place it anywhere on the workspace with a left click. We need to change the settings on the second stack like below:

1. Change "point in direction 90" to -90

2. Change "go to x: -213 y: -123" to 216 and -123

3. Change "change x by 2" to -2

After the stacks are adjusted, put "when ⚑ clicked" block from the "Events" options in the Code tab at the top of the entire stack. When you are done, the entire stack would look like this:

```
when [flag] clicked
point in direction 90
go to x: -213 y: -123
repeat until <touching edge?>
    change x by 2
end
point in direction -90
go to x: 216 y: -123
repeat until <touching edge?>
    change x by -2
end
```

This whole stack will help Avery move from one end of the street to the other, turn around and then walk to the street end she started from. It is a very cool project. Save it with the name "Fourth Project" so you can help Avery whenever needed.

Loop within a Loop

The last thing we will learn in this chapter is the secret of adding a loop block inside another loop block. Let's help Avery again because she wants to make at least 10 rounds on the street. Don't blame her, she wants to be healthy! We need to add one loop block to our Fourth Project and Avery will be able to walk up and down the city street.

We are going to use the loop#1 type and wrap most of the blocks inside them like shown in the image below. We are going to use 5 as the number of times the loop will execute.

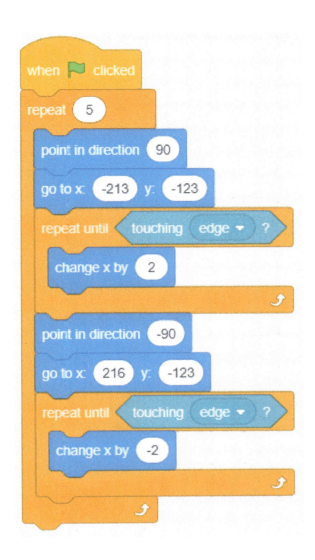

Chapter 6: Toy Box

Let's be real, you love toys. The truth is, every kid loves toys, even adults love toys! Your mom must have a box or container in your home where she puts all your toys once you are done playing with them.

Because there are toys in the box, we call it a toy box. If there are Legos in it, it is a Lego box. To be honest, that container can contain anything, even other stuff in the house. This is exactly how variables work. In programming, variables are used to store values. When we need to use the value, we use the variable. Later, if we want, we can change the value stored in the variable.

But, why are variables used? If we already have the value, why use a variable to access the value? Confusing isn't it? Well, the need for variables comes from another important part of programming - taking input from users. Remember when we talked about writing programs to take input and give output? The first part, taking inputs, will not be possible without a variable. The program will ask the user for input, and when the user gives input, the program will store it in a variable for future use.

In Scratch, there are three types of variables. What this actually means is we can store values in a variable in three ways. We can store a **number**, a **text** (usually called a **string** in programming), or a number of values called a **list**.

To understand the concept of variables, we will create and play the Gandalf the Wizard game! The rules of the game are simple. Gandalf is alone at his castle because all the student magicians are gone for holidays. Before leaving, the students played with Gandalf's belongings and left them scattered in the castle. Gandalf has to find them. Now, Saruman, who is the evil Wizard, has left some bad stuff in the castle that can really hurt Gandalf. Saruman also did a spell on Gandalf so he doesn't remember what belongings he's looking at. But, Gandalf does know he needs to find his stuff because he cannot do magic without them. Gandalf must gather his belongings without touching any bad things.

1. Create a new project and name it "Fifth Project".

2. Add a backdrop of "Castle 3" to the project.

3. Add the following sprites
    a. Wizard
    b. Wand
    c. Potion
    d. Wizard Hat
    e. Broom
4. Now, we have to create our variables "Lives" and "Power".
5. Change the size of all sprites to 50

All the blocks will be added to the Wizard sprite. Here is the screenshot of all blocks:

when 🏁 clicked
- go to x: -105 y: 133
- set Lives to 2
- set Power to 0

when right arrow key pressed
- change x by 10
- if touching Wand? then
  - change Power by 20
- if touching Wizard Hat? then
  - change Power by 20
- if touching Broom? then
  - change Lives by -1
  - set Power to 0
  - go to x: -105 y: 133
- if touching Potion? then
  - change Lives by -1
  - set Power to 0
  - go to x: -105 y: 133

when left arrow key pressed
- change x by -10
- if touching Wand? then
  - change Power by 20
- if touching Wizard Hat? then
  - change Power by 20
- if touching Broom? then
  - change Lives by -1
  - set Power to 0
  - go to x: -105 y: 133
- if touching Potion? then
  - change Lives by -1
  - set Power to 0
  - go to x: -105 y: 133

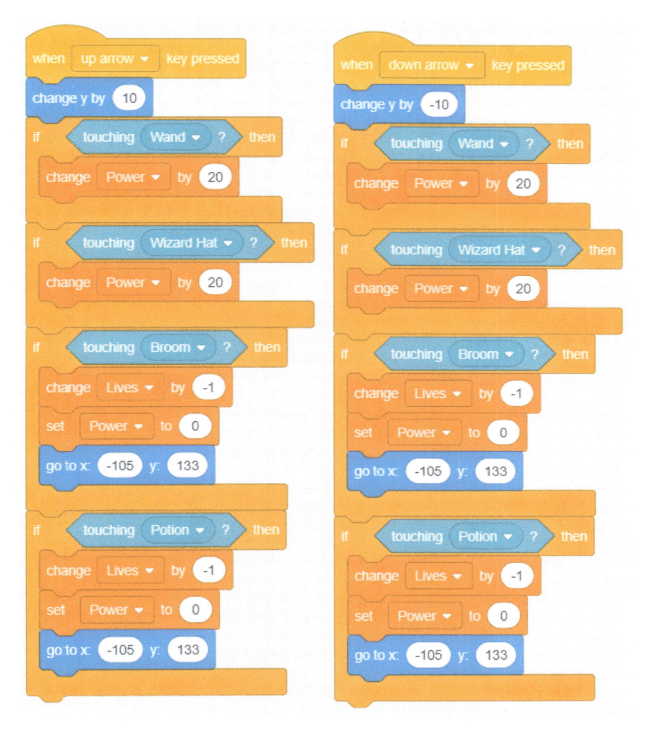

The block stack might look scary, but it's all very repetitive. We are trying to perform the same action for each ARROW key press. Let's start with the main block stack:

1. Add "when 🏁 clicked" block from the "Events" options in the Code tab.

2. Add "go to x:124 y:107" block from the "Motion" options in the Code tab. Change the x value to -105 and y value to 133.

3. Now, from the "Variables" option in the Code tab, drag "set LIVES to 0" to this stack. Change 0 to 2.

4. Now, from the "Variables" option in the Code tab, drag "set POWER to 0" to this stack.

Let's build the stack for the RIGHT ARROW key. We will just duplicate it for the rest of the ARROW keys.

1. Select "when SPACE key pressed" and change SPACE to RIGHT ARROW

2. Add "change x by 10" block

3. Add the IF block from "Control". Use the "sensing" block of "touching MOUSE-POINTER". Change MOUSE-POINTER to WAND. Inside this IF block, add a "Variables" block of "change LIVES by 1". Change LIVES to POWER and 1 to 20

4. Repeat Step 3 for Wizard Hat.

5. Repeat Step 3 for Broom. This time inside the IF block, adjust "change LIVES by 1" to "change LIVES by -1". Add blocks of "set LIVES to 0", and change LIVES to POWER. Also, add a "Motion" block of "go to x:124 y:107". Change the values to -105 and 133.

6. Repeat step 5 for Potion

This completes the stack for RIGHT ARROW. Repeat steps 1 to 6 for LEFT ARROW, DOWN ARROW and UP ARROW. The only difference would be in Step 2, where the value of x (or y) will be changed according to the direction of the arrow key, use the correct values. Refer to the screenshots provided earlier to make the correct changes for each stack.

The project is not complete. For example, ideally, when the LIVES become zero, the game should stop. But, to add such things will make the project very, very complicated. So, for now, let's work with this. Maybe think of this as a future project to improve this game. Gandalf will definitely love you for that!

Chapter 7: Breaking Stuff Is Good

My grandma used to say, "Soiled clothes are good!" whenever my mom scolded me for playing outside and making my clothes dirty. I really didn't understand how deep those words were. I used to be happy just because it meant mom didn't scold me anymore. When I grew up, I actually came to understand what my grandma meant. She was actually saying, "Mistakes are beautiful things a human can do." Why? Because mistakes help us grow and learn. Mistakes are what make us human!

Programmers learn faster by making mistakes. The human brain is a mysterious machine. It remembers mistakes for a long time. For all these reasons, I am going to encourage you to make mistakes and learn from them. Okay, here's a catch: there's making mistakes and there's being dumb. Don't do the second one kiddo, don't make mistakes just to make mistakes. Mistakes are only good if you make them while learning something. Don't forget.

Let's break some stuff in Scratch.

Data Race

Create a new project and name it "Sixth Project". We do not need to add any backdrop or sprites. In the "Variables" option under the Code tab, create a variable named "test". Make sure it is ticked in so the variable name and value show up on the stage. After that, create the following block stacks in the workspace:

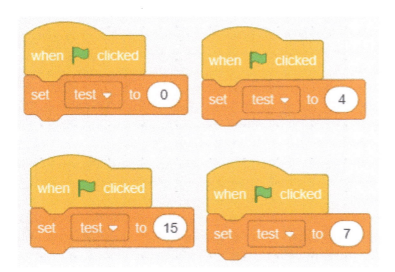

As you can see, we have multiple instances of the same blocks. In Scratch, since there is no fixed order of execution between different block stacks, in such circumstances, the result can be very unpredictable. Click on the green flag and let's see what the result is. For me, the result says test = 7.

Common sense says that since the block where test value is set to 7 is at the very bottom right side, maybe this block was executed the last, which is why the value of test is 7. Okay, that makes sense. Let's do an experiment. Swap the places of the block containing 7 with the block containing 15.

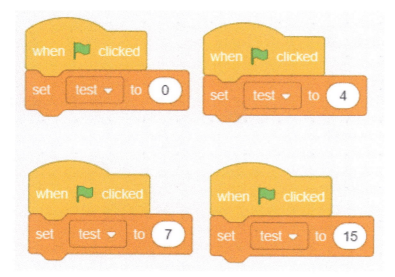

By our logic, when we run our project now, the test would have a value of 15 shown on the stage. Okay, running the project, what happens? The value of the test variable is still

7! But, that does not make sense. So, why is this happening, and can we predict what will happen in such situations? The phenomenon is called data race in programming and no, we cannot predict what will be the value of test variable when we run this project. It can change every time, or it can remain the same even if we change the order of block stacks (as we already experimented). There are a few guidelines to avoid this situation.

1. Avoid having more than one green flag block in your project. Combine other blocks under the one green flag block to ensure a consistent execution flow.

2. If there is no way to avoid this, use the wait function to delay execution of subsequent green flag blocks.

3. Use the Scratch broadcast feature. This allows you to broadcast execution progress on one sprite to other sprites so their blocks can be executed. This is one of the best ways to avoid clash resulting in data race. We are going to use this in a project in later chapters.

Variable Attribution

This is a very difficult concept to understand, detect and fix. When you create a new variable, Scratch asks if the variable should be linked to all sprites in the project, or linked to just the one selected under the "sprites and backdrop" section. This will not be a problem in simpler projects where all the sprites are related to each other. In advanced projects, where you would like to create a group of sprites independent of each other, where variables related to one (group of) sprite should not be affected if another (group of) sprite is updated, correctly attributing with sprites is very crucial to getting correct results.

This is an advanced concept that is outside of the scope of this book. Once you have good experience with Scratch, you should come back to this topic.

Confusing Similar Blocks

Have you ever seen twin babies? It is a nightmare. No one can tell who is who, except maybe the mother. Twins look so similar that confusions are guaranteed.

There are many blocks in Scratch that look the same. Okay, that's bad. But do you know what's worse? There are many blocks that seem like they have the same functionality, but can result in totally different and unexpected results.

Let's delete all blocks from our Sixth Project and add a cat sprite to it. Choose any backdrop you want, it's entirely optional. Add the following block stack to the cat sprite.

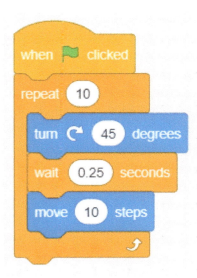

Run this project and you will see the cat rotate but remain in the same position! The cat should have moved somewhere but it didn't. That's because this "move 10 steps" motion block is direction-dependent. It means the sprite will move 10 steps in the direction it's facing. Since our sprite is also rotating, at the end the overall displacement becomes zero (this is actually a practical demonstration of a very important physics concept).

What we really wanted was the cat rotating yet moving in a straight horizontal line, like the cat is rolling on the floor! Hmmm, so how can we do that? If you look at the blocks available under the "Motions" option on the Code tab, you will see another block "change x by 10".

Replacing the block, adding some new blocks for better aesthetics and changing a few values of existing ones, the updated stack looks like this.

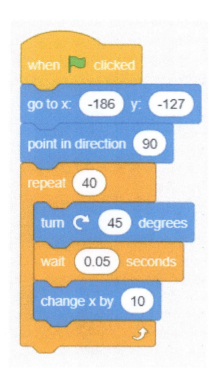

Now, let's run the project. Wow! The cat *does* look like it's rolling on the floor! And, it comes out on top every time. Cats are superior beings, it is proven!

Wrong Placement

The order of blocks is very crucial in some circumstances. Scratch generally executes the blocks with a top-down approach. It means the block at the top gets executed first, and the block at the bottom will be executed at the end. In the previous example, if we swap the position of "change x by 10" block and "turn 45 degrees", there will be no effect on the result.

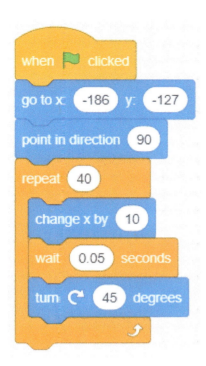

This gives the same output as previous stack

But, the order will matter in other circumstances. Remember Abby? She is in her bedroom and needs to go from her computer desk to her dressing table. Now, her bed is in the center, so she needs to walk around the bed. Can we write a program for Abby telling her the best route? Let's scratch.

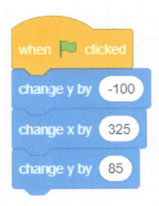

The above block stack will move Abby from her computer desk to the dressing table without bumping her into the bed. If you look closely, the order of "Motion" blocks is crucial because if we move Abby in a horizontal direction before moving her in a vertical direction, she'll bump into the bed. She has to travel in a U shape to avoid the bed.

In this chapter, we learned about the various errors you can face while programming with Scratch. We also discussed guidelines on how to avoid them. Remember, errors and mistakes challenge your creativity and are essential in your skill growth. Don't be afraid to take on the errors yourself. There is always a way out, Peter Pan!

Chapter 8: Cartoons Are Cool

Hey kiddo, we have discussed almost all the features of Scratch in the previous chapters. From here on, we are going to focus solely on creating fun projects without discussing the minor details of how things are working. The purpose is to show you the true power of Scratch. If it sounds too overwhelming, go back to previous chapters and practice with different blocks focusing on the input and output. Keen observation is key to learning new things.

In this chapter, I am going to give step-by-step instructions on how to create a short animation titled Max and Cheesy - our very own tribute to the famous Tom and Jerry cartoons. You will replicate the steps and watch the animation with friends and family.

Create a new project and name it "Seventh Project". Add a cat sprite, rename it Max and give it x and y values of -184 and -122.

We are going to use an extension to add sound effects to our animation. On the bottom left corner of the Scratch screen, you will see a unique icon with a plus sign. With this option, we can add advanced extensions that help in creating animations and games.

Choose the first option of "text to speech".

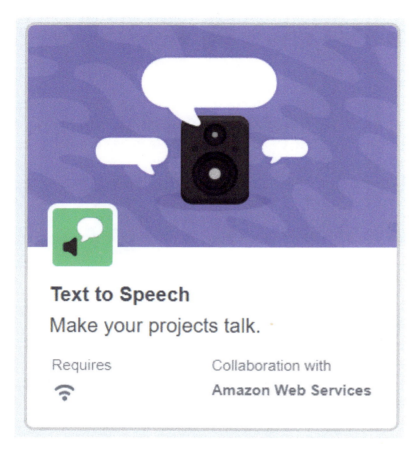

This extension adds some blocks that will help us convert text into speech. We can also add background music to our animation.

We are going to add the following three sprites to our project:

1. Cat, rename it to Max
2. Mouse, rename it to Cheesy
3. Puppy, rename it to Rocky

We can take advantage of the huge library available directly through Scratch. When Max is selected, go to the "Sounds" tab. Towards the bottom-left corner of the screen, you will see the following icon. Click on the search icon and you will see a catalogue of sounds.

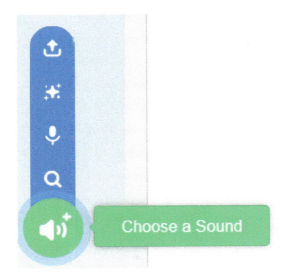

Click on the "Loop" and then select the "Mystery" music.

Let's go back to the Code tab and start using the blocks.

Select the Max sprite and add the blocks in the following order.

The "set voice to tenor" and "set language to English" will be available under the "Text to Speech" option of the Code tab.

The next stack for Max is given below.

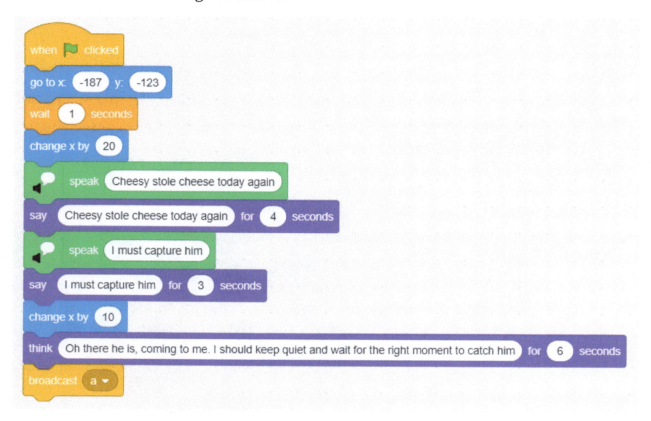

The only new thing we have used in this stack is the broadcast block. It is present in the "Events" option under the Code tab. The purpose of broadcast is to transfer control to another sprite. The remaining blocks for Max are given below.

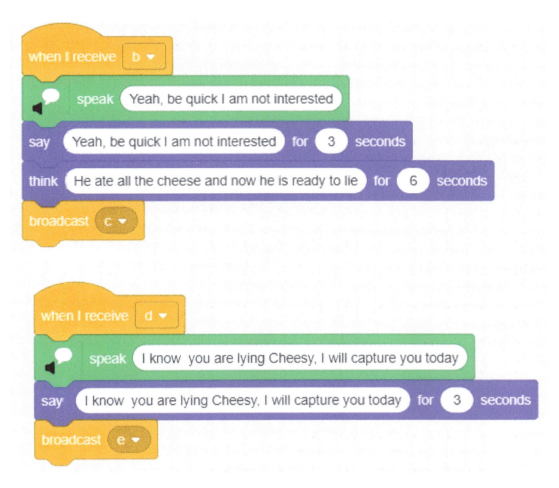

Note how the speak and say blocks are grouped together to create a subtitles effect along with the speech. The last block stack for Max is:

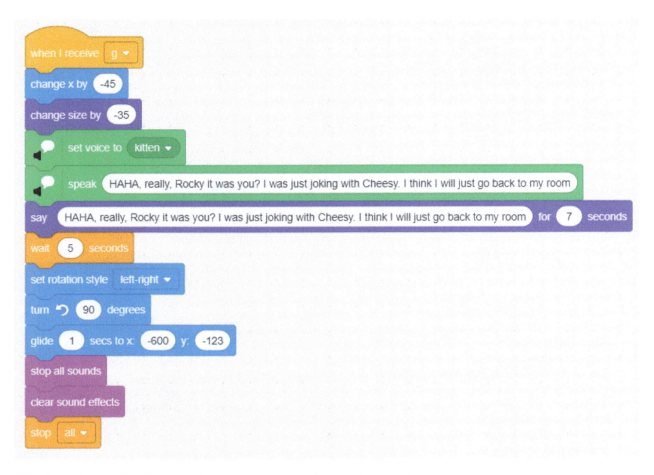

The last three blocks end the execution of the entire project.

The blocks for Cheesy are given below. Select Cheesy in the "sprites and backdrop" area and create the block stack.

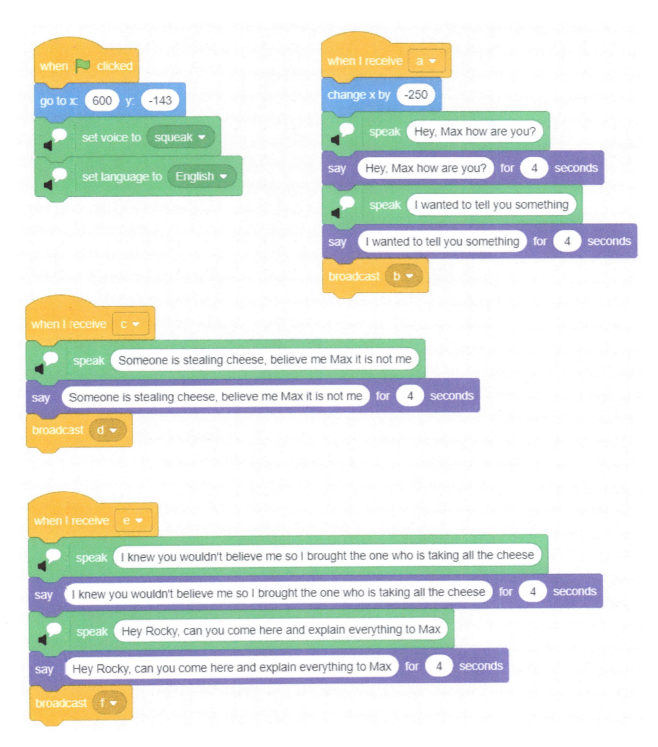

The block stack for Rocky is given next.

The last thing to do is to add a backdrop to our project. I have used the "Room 2" backdrop, but you can use something else if you want to.

As you can see from the screenshots, we have relied heavily on broadcasts to transfer execution flow from one sprite to another. One new "Motion" block that's used in this project is the "glide". Glide block moves the sprite in a rather smooth fashion instead of jumping it to a specific position (which is what "go to x: y:" block does). I have used both Motion blocks in this project so you can note the difference between their usage and results.

Chapter 9: Let's Dance

We have just completed a very big project, so, it is time to dance! We are going to create a dance party in Scratch.

Let's start by creating a new project and naming it "Eighth Project". We are going to use the backdrop of "spotlight". Let's add a bunch of dancers to the dance floor, namely the sprites of Anina Dance, Cassy Dance, Jouvi Dance, LB Dance, D-Money Dance and Ten80 Dance.

Since we are using dance sprites, the "Dance Magic" sound will automatically be added to the library. Dancing is easy, and so is creating the blocks to have a Scratch dance party.

The following block stack is created to play a continuous loop of music.

Now, the following block stack must be added to all sprites. It will enable all of them to move to the music.

And, that's it! You must be wondering why such an easy project? Well, because everyone deserves some fun. Giving your mind a break is very essential to make sure the creative processes are not overloaded. A mind free from thoughts, pressures and expectations is much more creative. And, also, dancing with friends is fun, liberating and great exercise! You should have dance parties with your friends in real-life. It might sound scary but it is not. Nothing, and I repeat nothing can beat dancing with your friends to the tune of 80s disco music while drinking kool-aid! Give it a try as soon as possible.

After completing such an easy project, your mind will already be hungry for the next big challenge. Well that's how Peter Pan thrives, and the next chapter will have plenty of complex things to solve with a creative touch.

Chapter 10: Become A Scientist

Up till now we have used Scratch to create animations, have dance parties, and all kinds of fun. The capabilities of Scratch do not end there. We can use Scratch for very advanced and serious applications. The next two projects in this book deal with science and mathematics. They are moderately challenging because the main focus is to show how versatile Scratch is.

The Calculator

Yes, we are going to create a simple calculator that takes two numbers and performs addition, multiplication, division and subtraction.

We start with a new project, naming it "Ninth Project". We do not need a backdrop or sprite, but we can leave the cat sprite as is, it is up to you.

In this project, we are going to use operators with variables. We also use a new input method available in the "Sensing" option under the Code tab.

We start building the block stack with the "when ⚑ clicked" block.

1. Add "when ⚑ clicked" block from the "Events" options in the Code tab.

2. Create six variables "num1", "num2", "add", "sub", "mul" and "div" using the "create variable" block in the "Variables" option

3. Use the ask block from the "Sensing" option to take the first number as input

4. Use the "set" block to store this input to num1 variable

5. Repeat steps 3 and 4 for num2

6. Use the set block for addition. This time use the addition operator from the "Operators" option under Code tab with the two variables num1 and num2.

7. Repeat step 6 for subtraction, multiplication and division, each time choosing the relevant operator with the set block.

8. In the "Variables" option, make sure num1 and num2 are unchecked while the remaining four variables are checked to show on the stage.

Our calculator is ready. The block stack will look like this.

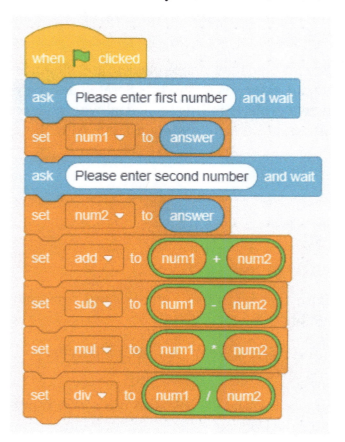

It is a fully functional calculator. Can you add any new features to this calculator? Maybe add more operations such as logical operators (comparison, etc.). Maybe add a loop so the user keeps using calculator until they press a specific keyboard key. Take it as the next challenge.

The first program I wrote was in BASIC language and it was a simple calculator. I had to add a lot of code to handle division by zero issues and other problems. Try division by zero on your new Scratch calculator. See if it breaks the calculator or you get answers that make sense. Also try very large numbers and very small numbers. Check the performance of the calculator. If you want to test the capability of a project, you need to throw things at it that no one ever thought about. After building a project, your aim should be to try and do everything to break it. It will make your thought process even more creative. You will think of stuff you didn't think about when creating the project.

Let us move to our next and last project of this book.

The Magician

Yes, you can become a magician by using Scratch! Our next project, that we will name "Tenth Project", asks you to choose a number between 0 and 31. It then asks you several questions until it successfully finds the number you chose! This is pure magic, done with the help of mathematics.

The block stack is given on the next page. We have created a variable with the name "number" to store user input. The user replies either "yes" or "no" to our questions. Truth be told, the whole magic trick is just a good understanding of numbers and counting. There is no need for a sprite or backdrop, but you can add if you want to.

1. Add "when ⚑ clicked" block from the "Events" options in the Code tab.
2. Add the variable "number" and set its value to zero
3. Start taking input from the user by asking if the number they have picked is an odd number. If yes, increase the value of variable number by 1
4. Repeat the questions four more times. Each time the user answers yes, increase the number by the next power of 2 else the variable value stays the same.
5. Provide the correctly guessed number to the user.
6. Do a cool stunt like a real magician as the user keeps wondering how you guessed the number correctly!

In this project, we have used one new block, which is "join". This block is used to join multiple strings together usually before showing as output to the user.

You might have noticed how Scratch automatically detects the best data type to use in a situation. There is no need to explicitly convert data types. On the other hand, in many other programming languages, the programmer is required to take care of any data conversions.

```
when [flag] clicked
set [number ▼] to (0)
say [Pick a number from 0-31.] for (3) seconds
ask [Is your number an odd number?] and wait
if <(answer) = (yes)> then
    change [number ▼] by (1)
end
ask [Is your number in this set: 2, 3, 6, 7, 10, 11, 14, 15, 18, 19, 22, 23, 26, 27, 30, 31?] and wait
if <(answer) = (yes)> then
    change [number ▼] by (2)
end
ask [Is your number in this set: 4, 5, 6, 7, 12, 13, 14, 15, 20, 21, 22, 23, 28, 29, 30, 31?] and wait
if <(answer) = (yes)> then
    change [number ▼] by (4)
end
ask [Is your number in this set: 8, 9, 10, 11, 12, 13, 14, 15, 24, 25, 26, 27, 28, 29, 30, 31?] and wait
if <(answer) = (yes)> then
    change [number ▼] by (8)
end
ask [Is your number in this set: 16, 17, 18, 19, 20, 21, 22, 23, 24, 25, 26, 27, 28, 29, 30, 31?] and wait
if <(answer) = (yes)> then
    change [number ▼] by (16)
end
say (join [Your number is ] (number)) for (5) seconds
```

Advanced Concepts

After completing more than 10 projects in this book, it is time to focus on a few concepts in theory. We are going to discuss some advanced things here kiddo, but you can do it! Believe me, even many adults find these concepts hard to grasp.

Scratch is one of a kind when it comes to programming techniques. In Scratch, you use blocks to solve problems and create new things, an approach called block-oriented programming. Do you know what the most popular programming languages are? According to Stackify, here's the top three from 2019:

1. Java
2. C
3. Python

Guess what? None of them use block-oriented programming. There are other approaches to programming, and we are going to discuss them now.

Functional Programming

Functional programming revolves around, drum roll please, functions! Remember our "Fifth Project", where we helped Gandalf find his magic stuff? We duplicated the same set of blocks for all the four arrow keys. It was not very efficient, was it? Creating functions is a way to cut down the number of blocks (or number of script lines) and avoid repetition.

How do we do that? We identify the line of codes that we will be using more than once. We give it a function name so whenever we need to execute it, we just call that name. There's one other amazing thing about functions. You can give them input (multiple if you can) and they return an output. A real-life example is a washing machine. You put in clothes, liquid detergent, and sometimes coins. The machine also takes water from an intake and washes all the clothes. After a preset amount of time, the machine gives you the clothes washed, rinsed and sometimes dried. Keep in mind that a washing machine can wash different types of clothes.

It would not be wrong to say that functions are mini programs within the main program. Breaking a big program into smaller functions also improves readability. But, sometimes it can make it harder to understand the flow of the program. The key is to identify if there's a need for a function.

Twist

Now, here's a twist. You can create a block in Scratch that behaves like a function. How do you do that? This is something you will have to learn after you become good at things we have covered in this book. For now, add this to your to-do list.

Object-Oriented Programming

This is another type of programming, where everything is considered an object. Variables, constants, and even functions are just objects, or part of an object. This concept is closest to real-life and most applications built to tackle real-life problems are built using this approach.

Now, let us take the example of Cooper, the dog. He has many characteristics: he's (super) cute, friendly, talkative, happy and lovable. When it comes to doing stuff (actions), he can wag his tail, jump, walk, eat, hug, kiss, and lick among many other things. In the world of programming, Cooper is an object. His characteristics are called attributes. His actions are called modules (a fancy word for functions). We can give the object instructions to get some output.

We can also use, change, and transfer the available attributes. I know there's a saying you can't teach an old dog new tricks, but Cooper is a young fellow and we can definitely teach him some new tricks. This is equivalent to adding new modules to an object.

Algorithms and Flowcharts

When you advance in programming, you will see that it is difficult to keep up with the details and flow when a code starts to grow big. To help programmers keep track of everything, there is an entire process used when writing complex programs. Programmers write what is called an algorithm before writing the actual code.

An algorithm is a list of instructions that is written before coding is started. It helps break down the problem into groups of actions. Algorithms are actually used to detail the solution of the problem in simple human language. It also helps programmers to remain on task because sometimes it's easy to lose focus. Algorithms can be written for any task. For example, write a step-by-step guide on how to get ready for school in the morning.

Although not as popular anymore, veteran programmers still work with a flowchart, mostly to show non-technical colleagues how the program/application will be created. This is a bit more technical than writing algorithms because the shapes used to represent each step must match the type of action happening in that step. But, this makes much more sense to view a flowchart because it gives a clear understanding of the flow of a program. Flowcharts are also used by planning teams to lay out a plan. If you have used MS Excel, you might have seen the flowchart section when you opened the Insert Shapes menu.

Health is Happiness

Why are we talking about health? Because health does matter. Talk with an old person and they'll tell you health is the most precious thing in this world. Here's a secret for you kiddo: if you have health, you can do anything. Spending a lot of time in front of screens can lead to various health concerns, especially those related to the eyes. In today's world, kids are also not spending too much time outdoors. It may lead to weaker muscles and immune system.

I am going to tell you a few tips that you can follow to keep your health in top condition.

The 20-second Rule

The rule is simple: for every 20 minutes spent in front of a computer, cellphone or a tablet screen, you should look at an object that's 20 feet away for 20 seconds. Why is that a good idea? Because you use your eye muscles to focus on a certain object. When you focus on a nearby object, your eye muscles remain strained. If you keep looking for a long time, the muscles get tired. It is for this reason that your eyes feel weary after spending a couple of hours looking at a handheld device. When you look at an object that's far away, your eye muscles get time to relax. This will help you a lot because many adults spend around 15 hours of each day in front of a screen. It is possible you would be doing the same when you grow up even when you don't want to. This is because of work requirements. The 20-second rule will help you avoid strained and sore eyes.

Hydration is Key

How much fluid do you drink in a day? The best fluid you can drink is water, because it has no bad stuff such as sugar. Using a computer or handheld smart device is fun and many times distracting. You lose focus and sense of time. This can lead to reduced hunger and thirst which is very bad for your health. What we can do is whenever you take the break for the 20-second rule, drink some water. Now, everyone has different requirements depending upon their age. Ask an adult how much water you should drink in a day.

When you start drinking more water, you will need to pee more. This feels like a nuisance but is very crucial to clean your body. Do not hold up, you should go to the bathroom as soon as you feel the need to do so.

When I talk about hydration, it's not just about drinking fluids. Your eyes also require good hydration levels for proper function. Have you ever experienced redness or itching after spending a long time in front of a screen? The phenomenon is pretty unique. Do you know why you blink? Blinking is an automatic process where your body removes dust and other things from the eyes and rehydrates the eyes. Have you ever noticed that sometimes when you are focusing on a screen, you forget to blink and only realize it after a few minutes? When you don't blink, the dust doesn't get cleaned up and rehydration also doesn't happen. In short, don't forget to blink.

Running and Exercise

You might already be active enough, but make sure you allocate enough time for physical activities. When you sit for a long time, the muscles in your legs become weaker. The joints also lose their strength. These will take a long time to happen and that's why these are very dangerous. You will slowly slip into a routine and when you start to notice the bad things, the internal damage might already be beyond repair. Stretching exercises are a great way of relaxing muscles. I know it sounds wrong, but stretching does relax the muscles. A doctor can give a good answer on how it works.

Going out also changes your perspective. It is a great way to relax your mind so it can get out of pressure situations. Sometimes when you think too hard for too long, the creative process gets stuck. In such situations, it is good to take a break, go outside to play or run.

Now, I understand that as a kid it is very difficult to go outside because you need permission and company. That's not a bad thing kiddo, trust me. Talk with your parents and let them know you need some of their time so they can go out with you. It is not like going out for a vacation. It won't require a lot of preparation. 20 to 30 minutes a day is good enough. It will give everyone some more time together and it will also benefit your parents' health.

Perfect Posture

There is a good way and a bad way to do every job in this world. Many people do things the wrong way because it's just easier. Using computers and handheld devices with the wrong posture is also another very easy pitfall to fall into. There are many parts of your body that cannot handle stress for a long period of time. These parts include your neck, your wrists, your spine, and ankles.

When you sit in front of a computer, make sure of following things:

1. Your feet are grounded firmly on the floor
2. Your thighs should be parallel to the floor
3. Your calves should be perpendicular to the floor
4. Your back should be relaxed and have a natural arc. The chair should provide support to your back but must not push into it
5. The computer table should be on the same height as your arms
6. The computer screen should be on the same height as your eyes
7. The mouse should be light-weight
8. Keyboard should be soft-touch so you don't need to press them hard

I know these are a lot of rules. But, they are very important. It will take time to follow all of them without effort. It also means you have to use the right kind of furniture. Again, that's not something you will be able to do yourself. Understandably, this is again something you should discuss with your parents. Chances are they already know about these but are not following them. Tell them the importance and the problems that can happen if you don't follow them for a long time.

Project Ideas

I know you want to work on more exciting, fun projects. Well, a book can't have everything even if I try my best. Now, I am going to discuss a few projects that you should work on. I am confident they will further challenge your creativity and you will love them.

Suggested Project #1

Create a Text Generator

Text is just a combination of words put in the right order. Create a text generator that creates an application to take leave from school. The project will take input following information from the user:

- Name
- Name of school
- Current date
- Start and end dates for the leave
- User can select a reason from the following options:
    - Sickness
    - Going to a relative
    - Preparing for a test
    - Sports competition

The body of the letter must have the correct wording depending upon the reason the user chooses for the leave.

Suggested Project #2

Balloon Popper

Have you popped balloons at a birthday party? It's exciting, scary and fun at the same time. In this project, you have to create a game where the balloons are falling from above and you have to pop them before they pass the bottom of the screen. There is a one minute timer and the game will stop after it is over. Each balloon popped will add

10 points to the score. There should be constant music playing in the background. A pop sound should be played when a balloon is popped.

There are no levels, so balloons will always fall at the same speed and the timer is always set to one minute. It is a game that is more fun when challenging your friends taking turns. Whoever scores the most points will win.

Suggested Project #3

Cheese Wheel

Guide Marty, the mouse, to the cheese wheel. Players start with three lives. The player should be able to use the arrow keys to guide the mouse to the cheese without touching the sides of the tunnels. The tunnel walls are laced with poison, and touching the tunnel wall once will decrease lives by one.

There will be three levels to the game. In each level, there must be a new tunnel map, each harder than the previous one. The size of the mouse will also increase by 10 for added difficulty.

Suggested Project #4

Minesweeper

Windows used to come with a very cool game called Minesweeper. Unfortunately, Windows 10 doesn't have it anymore. Good thing is, we can create minesweeper using Scratch. How is the game played? Well, the game starts with square cells, each with hidden content. You have to click on a cell to reveal its content. Some cells contain a mine. If you click on a cell and it reveals a mine, the game is over. Revealing each cell without touching a mine adds to your total score. You need to reveal all cells in a specific amount of time. Each cell has a number, which tells how many mines there are in its neighborhood. Note that a square can have nine neighbors at maximum.

Now, it might not look like it, but this game is very thrilling and fun. There's also a timer so you can see how much time it took for you to clear the field. The timer doesn't affect the outcome, it is just for bragging rights.

There will be 3 difficulty levels which can be chosen at the start of the game. Each level has a bigger field and more mines. On the other hand, clearing each cell on a higher difficulty gets you more points. When one difficult level is completed, the player should be asked if they want to continue to the next level.

To place mines randomly on the field, you can use the randomizer block available in Scratch.

The three projects have varying difficulty in terms of building. If you are not able to complete them, do not be discouraged. You can find many project ideas on the Scratch website. Focus on that and once you are ready, come back to these.

Conclusion

Congratulations Peter Pan, you have graduated from the Nat University of Scratching! Rejoice, but remember, your journey in the creative world has just started. There are hundreds of YouTube tutorials on Scratch from which you can get advanced training. Your time given to Scratch is a great investment. It will pay off a lot in the future.

And, truth be told, it's not just about the future. How cool will it be when you show your projects to your friends and challenge them to beat you at it? You already know you are so good at it. Yet, everything becomes better when you have others to enjoy it with.

As a parent or guardian to a kid, it is crucial to keep encouraging your kid to take on new challenges. Kids thrive in difficult situations. Now, there's a breaking point for every human. So, it is your duty to monitor your kid's progress and make sure they are not pushed beyond their limits. Kids might not understand this fact and will feel frustrated.

Whenever you feel stuck, make sure you do not give up. Soldier on Peter Pan, for great success lies beyond the storm of hardship. I wish you the best of luck in your journey. I can guarantee it will be full of excitement, joy and adventure. After all, I used to be *the* Peter Pan back in the day!

CPSIA information can be obtained
at www.ICGtesting.com
Printed in the USA
BVHW010424210123
656715BV00017BA/1243